T0249132

A Dome of
Many-Coloured
Glass

A Dome of Many-Coloured Glass

Amy Lowell

MINT EDITIONS

A Dome of Many-Coloured Glass was first published in 1912.

This edition published by Mint Editions 2021.

ISBN 9781513132488

Published by Mint Editions®

MINT
EDITIONS

minteditionbooks.com

Publishing Director: Jennifer Newens
Design & Production: Rachel Lopez Metzger
Project Manager: Micaela Clark
Typesetting: Westchester Publishing Services

Contents

LYRICAL POEMS

Before the Altar

Before the Altar, bowed, he stands
With empty hands;
Upon it perfumed offerings burn
Wreathing with smoke the sacrificial urn.
Not one of all these has he given,
No flame of his has leapt to Heaven
Firesouled, vermilion-hearted,
Forked, and darted,
Consuming what a few spare pence
Have cheaply bought, to fling from hence
In idly-asked petition.

His sole condition
Love and poverty.
And while the moon
Swings slow across the sky,
Athwart a waving pine tree,
And soon
Tips all the needles there
With silver sparkles, bitterly
He gazes, while his soul
Grows hard with thinking of the poorness of his dole.

"Shining and distant Goddess, hear my prayer
Where you swim in the high air!
With charity look down on me,
Under this tree,
Tending the gifts I have not brought,
The rare and goodly things
I have not sought.
Instead, take from me all my life!

"Upon the wings
Of shimmering moonbeams
I pack my poet's dreams
For you.

My wearying strife,
My courage, my loss,
Into the night I toss
For you.
Golden Divinity,
Deign to look down on me
Who so unworthily
Offers to you:
All life has known,
Seeds withered unsown,
Hopes turning quick to fears,
Laughter which dies in tears.
The shredded remnant of a man
Is all the span
And compass of my offering to you.

"Empty and silent, I
Kneel before your pure, calm majesty.
On this stone, in this urn
I pour my heart and watch it burn,
Myself the sacrifice; but be
Still unmoved: Divinity."

From the altar, bathed in moonlight,
The smoke rose straight in the quiet night.

Suggested by the Cover of a Volume of Keats's Poems

Wild little bird, who chose thee for a sign
To put upon the cover of this book?
Who heard thee singing in the distance dim,
The vague, far greenness of the enshrouding wood,
When the damp freshness of the morning earth
Was full of pungent sweetness and thy song?

Who followed over moss and twisted roots,
And pushed through the wet leaves of trailing vines
Where slanting sunbeams gleamed uncertainly,
While ever clearer came the dropping notes,
Until, at last, two widening trunks disclosed
Thee singing on a spray of branching beech,
Hidden, then seen; and always that same song
Of joyful sweetness, rapture incarnate,
Filled the hushed, rustling stillness of the wood?

We do not know what bird thou art. Perhaps
That fairy bird, fabled in island tale,
Who never sings but once, and then his song
Is of such fearful beauty that he dies
From sheer exuberance of melody.

For this they took thee, little bird, for this
They captured thee, tilting among the leaves,
And stamped thee for a symbol on this book.
For it contains a song surpassing thine,
Richer, more sweet, more poignant. And the poet
Who felt this burning beauty, and whose heart
Was full of loveliest things, sang all he knew
A little while, and then he died; too frail
To bear this untamed, passionate burst of song.

APPLES OF HESPERIDES

Glinting golden through the trees,
    Apples of Hesperides!
Through the moon-pierced warp of night
Shoot pale shafts of yellow light,
Swaying to the kissing breeze
Swings the treasure, golden-gleaming,
    Apples of Hesperides!

Far and lofty yet they glimmer,
    Apples of Hesperides!
Blinded by their radiant shimmer,
Pushing forward just for these;
Dew-besprinkled, bramble-marred,
Poor duped mortal, travel-scarred,
Always thinking soon to seize
And possess the golden-glistening
    Apples of Hesperides!

Orbed, and glittering, and pendent,
    Apples of Hesperides!
Not one missing, still transcendent,
Clustering like a swarm of bees.
Yielding to no man's desire,
Glowing with a saffron fire,
Splendid, unassailed, the golden
    Apples of Hesperides!

Azure and Gold

April had covered the hills
    With flickering yellows and reds,
The sparkle and coolness of snow
    Was blown from the mountain beds.

Across a deep-sunken stream
    The pink of blossoming trees,
And from windless appleblooms
    The humming of many bees.

The air was of rose and gold
    Arabesqued with the song of birds
Who, swinging unseen under leaves,
    Made music more eager than words.

Of a sudden, aslant the road,
    A brightness to dazzle and stun,
A glint of the bluest blue,
    A flash from a sapphire sun.

Blue-birds so blue, 't was a dream,
    An impossible, unconceived hue,
The high sky of summer dropped down
    Some rapturous ocean to woo.

Such a colour, such infinite light!
    The heart of a fabulous gem,
Many-faceted, brilliant and rare.
    Centre Stone of the earth's diadem!
    .   .   .   .   .

Centre Stone of the Crown of the World,
    "Sincerity" graved on your youth!
And your eyes hold the blue-bird flash,
    The sapphire shaft, which is truth.

Petals

Life is a stream
On which we strew
Petal by petal the flower of our heart;
The end lost in dream,
They float past our view,
We only watch their glad, early start.

Freighted with hope,
Crimsoned with joy,
We scatter the leaves of our opening rose;
Their widening scope,
Their distant employ,
We never shall know. And the stream as it flows
Sweeps them away,
Each one is gone
Ever beyond into infinite ways.
We alone stay
While years hurry on,
The flower fared forth, though its fragrance still stays.

Venetian Glass

As one who sails upon a wide, blue sea
Far out of sight of land, his mind intent
Upon the sailing of his little boat,
On tightening ropes and shaping fair his course,
Hears suddenly, across the restless sea,
The rhythmic striking of some towered clock,
And wakes from thoughtless idleness to time:
Time, the slow pulse which beats eternity!
So through the vacancy of busy life
At intervals you cross my path and bring
The deep solemnity of passing years.
For you I have shed bitter tears, for you
I have relinquished that for which my heart
Cried out in selfish longing. And tonight
Having just left you, I can say: "'T is well.
Thank God that I have known a soul so true,
So nobly just, so worthy to be loved!"

FATIGUE

Stupefy my heart to every day's monotony,
    Seal up my eyes, I would not look so far,
Chasten my steps to peaceful regularity,
    Bow down my head lest I behold a star.

Fill my days with work, a thousand calm necessities
    Leaving no moment to consecrate to hope,
Girdle my thoughts within the dull circumferences
    Of facts which form the actual in one short hour's scope.

Give me dreamless sleep, and loose night's power over me,
    Shut my ears to sounds only tumultuous then,
Bid Fancy slumber, and steal away its potency,
    Or Nature wakes and strives to live again.

Let each day pass, well ordered in its usefulness,
    Unlit by sunshine, unscarred by storm;
Dower me with strength and curb all foolish eagerness—
    The law exacts obedience. Instruct, I will conform.

A Japanese Wood-Carving

High up above the open, welcoming door
It hangs, a piece of wood with colours dim.
Once, long ago, it was a waving tree
And knew the sun and shadow through the leaves
Of forest trees, in a thick eastern wood.
The winter snows had bent its branches down,
The spring had swelled its buds with coming flowers,
Summer had run like fire through its veins,
While autumn pelted it with chestnut burrs,
And strewed the leafy ground with acorn cups.
Dark midnight storms had roared and crashed among
Its branches, breaking here and there a limb;
But every now and then broad sunlit days
Lovingly lingered, caught among the leaves.
Yes, it had known all this, and yet to us
It does not speak of mossy forest ways,
Of whispering pine trees or the shimmering birch;
But of quick winds, and the salt, stinging sea!
An artist once, with patient, careful knife,
Had fashioned it like to the untamed sea.
Here waves uprear themselves, their tops blown back
By the gay, sunny wind, which whips the blue
And breaks it into gleams and sparks of light.
Among the flashing waves are two white birds
Which swoop, and soar, and scream for very joy
At the wild sport. Now diving quickly in,
Questing some glistening fish. Now flying up,
Their dripping feathers shining in the sun,
While the wet drops like little glints of light,
Fall pattering backward to the parent sea.
Gliding along the green and foam-flecked hollows,
Or skimming some white crest about to break,
The spirits of the sky deigning to stoop
And play with ocean in a summer mood.
Hanging above the high, wide open door,

It brings to us in quiet, firelit room,
The freedom of the earth's vast solitudes,
Where heaping, sunny waves tumble and roll,
And seabirds scream in wanton happiness.

A Little Song

When you, my Dear, are away, away,
How wearily goes the creeping day.
A year drags after morning, and night
Starts another year of candle light.
O Pausing Sun and Lingering Moon!
Grant me, I beg of you, this boon.

Whirl round the earth as never sun
Has his diurnal journey run.
And, Moon, slip past the ladders of air
In a single flash, while your streaming hair
Catches the stars and pulls them down
To shine on some slumbering Chinese town.
O Kindly Sun! Understanding Moon!
Bring evening to crowd the footsteps of noon.

But when that long awaited day
Hangs ripe in the heavens, your voyaging stay.
Be morning, O Sun! with the lark in song,
Be afternoon for ages long.
And, Moon, let you and your lesser lights
Watch over a century of nights.

Behind a Wall

I own a solace shut within my heart,
 A garden full of many a quaint delight
 And warm with drowsy, poppied sunshine; bright,
Flaming with lilies out of whose cups dart
  Shining things
  With powdered wings.

Here terrace sinks to terrace, arbors close
 The ends of dreaming paths; a wanton wind
 Jostles the half-ripe pears, and then, unkind,
Tumbles a-slumber in a pillar rose,
  With content
  Grown indolent.

By night my garden is o'erhung with gems
 Fixed in an onyx setting. Fireflies
 Flicker their lanterns in my dazzled eyes.
In serried rows I guess the straight, stiff stems
  Of hollyhocks
  Against the rocks.

So far and still it is that, listening,
 I hear the flowers talking in the dawn;
 And where a sunken basin cuts the lawn,
Cinctured with iris, pale and glistening,
  The sudden swish
  Of a waking fish.

A Winter Ride

Who shall declare the joy of the running!
    Who shall tell of the pleasures of flight!
Springing and spurning the tufts of wild heather,
    Sweeping, wide-winged, through the blue dome of light.
Everything mortal has moments immortal,
    Swift and God-gifted, immeasurably bright.

So with the stretch of the white road before me,
    Shining snowcrystals rainbowed by the sun,
Fields that are white, stained with long, cool, blue shadows,
    Strong with the strength of my horse as we run.
Joy in the touch of the wind and the sunlight!
    Joy! With the vigorous earth I am one.

A Coloured Print by Shokei

It winds along the face of a cliff
    This path which I long to explore,
And over it dashes a waterfall,
    And the air is full of the roar
And the thunderous voice of waters which sweep
In a silver torrent over some steep.

It clears the path with a mighty bound
    And tumbles below and away,
And the trees and the bushes which grow in the rocks
    Are wet with its jewelled spray;
The air is misty and heavy with sound,
And small, wet wildflowers star the ground.

Oh! The dampness is very good to smell,
    And the path is soft to tread,
And beyond the fall it winds up and on,
    While little streamlets thread
Their own meandering way down the hill
Each singing its own little song, until

I forget that 't is only a pictured path,
    And I hear the water and wind,
And look through the mist, and strain my eyes
    To see what there is behind;
For it must lead to a happy land,
This little path by a waterfall spanned.

SONG

Oh! To be a flower
    Nodding in the sun,
Bending, then upspringing
    As the breezes run;
Holding up
A scent-brimmed cup,
    Full of summer's fragrance to the summer sun.

Oh! To be a butterfly
    Still, upon a flower,
Winking with its painted wings,
    Happy in the hour.
Blossoms hold
Mines of gold
    Deep within the farthest heart of each chaliced flower.

Oh! To be a cloud
    Blowing through the blue,
Shadowing the mountains,
    Rushing loudly through
Valleys deep
Where torrents keep
    Always their plunging thunder and their misty arch of blue.

Oh! To be a wave
    Splintering on the sand,
Drawing back, but leaving
    Lingeringly the land.
Rainbow light
Flashes bright
    Telling tales of coral caves half hid in yellow sand.

Soon they die, the flowers;
    Insects live a day;
Clouds dissolve in showers;
    Only waves at play

Last forever.
Shall endeavor
    Make a sea of purpose mightier than we dream today?

The Fool Errant

The Fool Errant sat by the highway of life
    And his gaze wandered up and his gaze wandered down,
A vigorous youth, but with no wish to walk,
    Yet his longing was great for the distant town.

He whistled a little frivolous tune
    Which he felt to be pulsing with ecstasy,
For he thought that success always followed desire,
    Such a very superlative fool was he.

A maiden came by on an ambling mule,
    Her gown was rose-red and her kerchief blue,
On her lap she carried a basket of eggs.
    Thought the fool, "There is certainly room for two."

So he jauntily swaggered towards the maid
    And put out his hand to the bridle-rein.
"My pretty girl," quoth the fool, "take me up,
    For to ride with you to the town I am fain."

But the maiden struck at his upraised arm
    And pelted him hotly with eggs, a score.
The mule, lashed into a fury, ran;
    The fool went back to his stone and swore.

Then out of the cloud of settling dust
    The burly form of an abbot appeared,
Reading his office he rode to the town.
    And the fool got up, for his heart was cheered.

He stood in the midst of the long, white road
    And swept off his cap till it touched the ground.
"Ah, Reverent Sir, well met," said the fool,
    "A worthier transport never was found.

"I pray you allow me to mount with you,
      Your palfrey seems both sturdy and young."
The abbot looked up from the holy book
      And cried out in anger, "Hold your tongue!

"How dare you obstruct the King's highroad,
      You saucy varlet, get out of my way."
Then he gave the fool a cut with his whip
      And leaving him smarting, he rode away.

The fool was angry, the fool was sore,
      And he cursed the folly of monks and maids.
"If I could but meet with a man," sighed the fool,
      "For a woman fears, and a friar upbraids."

Then he saw a flashing of distant steel
      And the clanking of harness greeted his ears,
And up the road journeyed knights-at-arms,
      With waving plumes and glittering spears.

The fool took notice and slowly arose,
      Not quite so sure was his foolish heart.
If priests and women would none of him
      Was it likely a knight would take his part?

They sang as they rode, these lusty boys,
      When one chanced to turn toward the highway's side,
"There's a sorry figure of fun," jested he,
      "Well, Sirrah! move back, there is scarce room to ride."

"Good Sirs, Kind Sirs," begged the crestfallen fool,
      "I pray of your courtesy speech with you,
I'm for yonder town, and have no horse to ride,
      Have you never a charger will carry two?"

Then the company halted and laughed out loud.
      "Was such a request ever made to a knight?"
"And where are your legs," asked one, "if you start,
      You may be inside the town gates tonight."

AMY LOWELL

"'T is a lazy fellow, let him alone,
    They've no room in the town for such idlers as he."
But one bent from his saddle and said, "My man,
    Art thou not ashamed to beg charity!

"Thou art well set up, and thy legs are strong,
    But it much misgives me lest thou'rt a fool;
For beggars get only a beggar's crust,
    Wise men are reared in a different school."

Then they clattered away in the dust and the wind,
    And the fool slunk back to his lonely stone;
He began to see that the man who asks
    Must likewise give and not ask alone.

Purple tree-shadows crept over the road,
    The level sun flung an orange light,
And the fool laid his head on the hard, gray stone
    And wept as he realized advancing night.

A great, round moon rose over a hill
    And the steady wind blew yet more cool;
And crouched on a stone a wayfarer sobbed,
    For at last he knew he was only a fool.

The Green Bowl

This little bowl is like a mossy pool
In a Spring wood, where dogtooth violets grow
Nodding in chequered sunshine of the trees;
A quiet place, still, with the sound of birds,
Where, though unseen, is heard the endless song
And murmur of the never resting sea.
'T was winter, Roger, when you made this cup,
But coming Spring guided your eager hand
And round the edge you fashioned young green leaves,
A proper chalice made to hold the shy
And little flowers of the woods. And here
They will forget their sad uprooting, lost
In pleasure that this circle of bright leaves
Should be their setting; once more they will dream
They hear winds wandering through lofty trees
And see the sun smiling between the leaves.

Hora Stellatrix

The stars hang thick in the apple tree,
The south wind smells of the pungent sea,
Gold tulip cups are heavy with dew.
The night's for you, Sweetheart, for you!
Starfire rains from the vaulted blue.

Listen! The dancing of unseen leaves.
A drowsy swallow stirs in the eaves.
Only a maiden is sorrowing.
'T is night and spring, Sweetheart, and spring!
Starfire lights your heart's blossoming.

In the intimate dark there's never an ear,
Though the tulips stand on tiptoe to hear,
So give; ripe fruit must shrivel or fall.
As you are mine, Sweetheart, give all!
Starfire sparkles, your coronal.

Fragment

What is poetry? Is it a mosaic
    Of coloured stones which curiously are wrought
    Into a pattern? Rather glass that's taught
By patient labor any hue to take
And glowing with a sumptuous splendor, make
    Beauty a thing of awe; where sunbeams caught,
    Transmuted fall in sheafs of rainbows fraught
With storied meaning for religion's sake.

Loon Point

Softly the water ripples
  Against the canoe's curving side,
Softly the birch trees rustle
  Flinging over us branches wide.

Softly the moon glints and glistens
  As the water takes and leaves,
Like golden ears of corn
  Which fall from loose-bound sheaves,

Or like the snow-white petals
  Which drop from an overblown rose,
When Summer ripens to Autumn
  And the freighted year must close.

From the shore come the scents of a garden,
  And between a gap in the trees
A proud white statue glimmers
  In cold, disdainful ease.

The child of a southern people,
  The thought of an alien race,
What does she in this pale, northern garden,
  How reconcile it with her grace?

But the moon in her wayward beauty
  Is ever and always the same,
As lovely as when upon Latmos
  She watched till Endymion came.

Through the water the moon writes her legends
  In light, on the smooth, wet sand;
They endure for a moment, and vanish,
  And no one may understand.

All round us the secret of Nature
    Is telling itself to our sight,
We may guess at her meaning but never
    Can know the full mystery of night.

But her power of enchantment is on us,
    We bow to the spell which she weaves,
Made up of the murmur of waves
    And the manifold whisper of leaves.

SUMMER

Some men there are who find in nature all
Their inspiration, hers the sympathy
Which spurs them on to any great endeavor,
To them the fields and woods are closest friends,
And they hold dear communion with the hills;
The voice of waters soothes them with its fall,
And the great winds bring healing in their sound.
To them a city is a prison house
Where pent up human forces labour and strive,
Where beauty dwells not, driven forth by man;
But where in winter they must live until
Summer gives back the spaces of the hills.
To me it is not so. I love the earth
And all the gifts of her so lavish hand:
Sunshine and flowers, rivers and rushing winds,
Thick branches swaying in a winter storm,
And moonlight playing in a boat's wide wake;
But more than these, and much, ah, how much more,
I love the very human heart of man.
Above me spreads the hot, blue mid-day sky,
Far down the hillside lies the sleeping lake
Lazily reflecting back the sun,
And scarcely ruffled by the little breeze
Which wanders idly through the nodding ferns.
The blue crest of the distant mountain, tops
The green crest of the hill on which I sit;
And it is summer, glorious, deep-toned summer,
The very crown of nature's changing year
When all her surging life is at its full.
To me alone it is a time of pause,
A void and silent space between two worlds,
When inspiration lags, and feeling sleeps,
Gathering strength for efforts yet to come.
For life alone is creator of life,
And closest contact with the human world
Is like a lantern shining in the night

To light me to a knowledge of myself.
I love the vivid life of winter months
In constant intercourse with human minds,
When every new experience is gain
And on all sides we feel the great world's heart;
The pulse and throb of life which makes us men!

"Tomorrow to Fresh Woods and Pastures New"

As for a moment he stands, in hardy masculine beauty,
Poised on the fircrested rock, over the pool which below him
Gleams in the wavering sunlight, waiting the shock of his plunging.
So for a moment I stand, my feet planted firm in the present,
Eagerly scanning the future which is so soon to possess me.

THE WAY

At first a mere thread of a footpath half blotted out by the grasses
Sweeping triumphant across it, it wound between hedges of roses
Whose blossoms were poised above leaves as pond lilies float on the
water,
While hidden by bloom in a hawthorn a bird filled the morning with
singing.

It widened a highway, majestic, stretching ever to distant horizons,
Where shadows of tree-branches wavered, vague outlines invaded by
sunshine;
No sound but the wind as it whispered the secrets of earth to the
flowers,
And the hum of the yellow bees, honey-laden and dusty with pollen.
And Summer said, "Come, follow onward, with no thought save the
longing to wander,
The wind, and the bees, and the flowers, all singing the great song of
Nature,
Are minstrels of change and of promise, they herald the joy of the
Future."

Later the solitude vanished, confused and distracted the road
Where many were seeking and jostling. Left behind were the trees
and the flowers,
The half-realized beauty of quiet, the sacred unconscious communing.
And now he is come to a river, a line of gray, sullen water,
Not blue and splashing, but dark, rolling somberly on to the ocean.
But on the far side is a city whose windows flame gold in the sunset.
It lies fair and shining before him, a gem set betwixt sky and water,
And spanning the river a bridge, frail promise to longing desire,
Flung by man in his infinite courage, across the stern force of the
water;
And he looks at the river and fears, the bridge is so slight, yet he
ventures
His life to its fragile keeping, if it fails the waves will engulf him.
O Arches! be strong to uphold him, and bear him across to the city,
The beautiful city whose spires still glow with the fires of sunset!

AMY LOWELL

Look, Dear, how bright the moonlight is tonight!
See where it casts the shadow of that tree
Far out upon the grass. And every gust
Of light night wind comes laden with the scent
Of opening flowers which never bloom by day:
Night-scented stocks, and four-o'clocks, and that
Pale yellow disk, upreared on its tall stalk,
The evening primrose, comrade of the stars.
It seems as though the garden which you love
Were like a swinging censer, its incense
Floating before us as a reverent act
To sanctify and bless our night of love.
Tell me once more you love me, that 't is you
Yes, really you, I touch, so, with my hand;
And tell me it is by your own free will
That you are here, and that you like to be
Just here, with me, under this sailing pine.
I need to hear it often for my heart
Doubts naturally, and finds it hard to trust.
Ah, Dearest, you are good to love me so,
And yet I would not have it goodness, rather
Excess of selfishness in you to need
Me through and through, as flowers need the sun.
I wonder can it really be that you
And I are here alone, and that the night
Is full of hours, and all the world asleep,
And none can call to you to come away;
For you have given all yourself to me
Making me gentle by your willingness.
Has your life too been waiting for this time,
Not only mine the sharpness of this joy?
Dear Heart, I love you, worship you as though
I were a priest before a holy shrine.
I'm glad that you are beautiful, although

Were you not lovely still I needs must love;
But you are all things, it must have been so
For otherwise it were not you. Come, close;
When you are in the circle of my arm
Faith grows a mountain and I take my stand
Upon its utmost top. Yes, yes, once more
Kiss me, and let me feel you very near
Wanting me wholly, even as I want you.
Have years behind been dark? Will those to come
Bring unguessed sorrows into our two lives?
What does it matter, we have had tonight!
Tonight will make us strong, for we believe
Each in the other, this is a sacrament.
Beloved, is it true?

AMY LOWELL

Roads

I know a country laced with roads,
    They join the hills and they span the brooks,
They weave like a shuttle between broad fields,
    And slide discreetly through hidden nooks.
They are canopied like a Persian dome
    And carpeted with orient dyes.
They are myriad-voiced, and musical,
    And scented with happiest memories.
O Winding roads that I know so well,
    Every twist and turn, every hollow and hill!
They are set in my heart to a pulsing tune
    Gay as a honey-bee humming in June.
'T is the rhythmic beat of a horse's feet
    And the pattering paws of a sheep-dog bitch;
'T is the creaking trees, and the singing breeze,
    And the rustle of leaves in the road-side ditch.

A cow in a meadow shakes her bell
    And the notes cut sharp through the autumn air,
Each chattering brook bears a fleet of leaves
    Their cargo the rainbow, and just now where
    The sun splashed bright on the road ahead
A startled rabbit quivered and fled.
    O Uphill roads and roads that dip down!
You curl your sun-spattered length along,
    And your march is beaten into a song
By the softly ringing hoofs of a horse
    And the panting breath of the dogs I love.
The pageant of Autumn follows its course
    And the blue sky of Autumn laughs above.

And the song and the country become as one,
    I see it as music, I hear it as light;
Prismatic and shimmering, trembling to tone,
    The land of desire, my soul's delight.

And always it beats in my listening ears
    With the gentle thud of a horse's stride,
With the swift-falling steps of many dogs,
    Following, following at my side.
O Roads that journey to fairyland!
    Radiant highways whose vistas gleam,
Leading me on, under crimson leaves,
    To the opaline gates of the Castles of Dream.

Teatro Bambino. Dublin, N. H.

How still it is! Sunshine itself here falls
    In quiet shafts of light through the high trees
Which, arching, make a roof above the walls
    Changing from sun to shadow as each breeze
Lingers a moment, charmed by the strange sight
Of an Italian theatre, storied, seer
    Of vague romance, and time's long history;
Where tiers of grass-grown seats sprinkled with white,
    Sweet-scented clover, form a broken sphere
    Grouped round the stage in hushed expectancy.

What sound is that which echoes through the wood?
    Is it the reedy note of an oaten pipe?
Perchance a minute more will see the brood
    Of the shaggy forest god, and on his lip
Will rest the rushes he is wont to play.
    His train in woven baskets bear ripe fruit
    And weave a dance with ropes of gray acorns,
So light their touch the grasses scarcely sway
    As they the measure tread to the lilting flute.
    Alas! 't is only Fancy thus adorns.

A cloud drifts idly over the shining sun.
    How damp it seems, how silent, still, and strange!
Surely 't was here some tragedy was done,
    And here the chorus sang each coming change?
Sure this is deep in some sweet, southern wood,
    These are not pines, but cypress tall and dark;
    That is no thrush which sings so rapturously,
But the nightingale in his most passionate mood
    Bursting his little heart with anguish. Hark!
    The tread of sandalled feet comes noiselessly.

The silence almost is a sound, and dreams
    Take on the semblances of finite things;

So potent is the spell that what but seems
    Elsewhere, is lifted here on Fancy's wings.
The little woodland theatre seems to wait,
    All tremulous with hope and wistful joy,
    For something that is sure to come at last,
Some deep emotion, satisfying, great.
    It grows a living presence, bold and shy,
    Cradling the future in a glorious past.

The Road to Avignon

A Minstrel stands on a marble stair,
Blown by the bright wind, debonair;
Below lies the sea, a sapphire floor,
Above on the terrace a turret door
Frames a lady, listless and wan,
But fair for the eye to rest upon.
The minstrel plucks at his silver strings,
And looking up to the lady, sings:—

>   Down the road to Avignon,
>   The long, long road to Avignon,
>   Across the bridge to Avignon,
>   One morning in the spring.

The octagon tower casts a shade
Cool and gray like a cutlass blade;
In sun-baked vines the cicalas spin,
The little green lizards run out and in.
A sail dips over the ocean's rim,
And bubbles rise to the fountain's brim.
The minstrel touches his silver strings,
And gazing up to the lady, sings:—

>   Down the road to Avignon,
>   The long, long road to Avignon,
>   Across the bridge to Avignon,
>   One morning in the spring.

Slowly she walks to the balustrade,
Idly notes how the blossoms fade
In the sun's caress; then crosses where
The shadow shelters a carven chair.
Within its curve, supine she lies,
And wearily closes her tired eyes.
The minstrel beseeches his silver strings,
And holding the lady spellbound, sings:—

>   Down the road to Avignon,
>   The long, long road to Avignon,

Across the bridge to Avignon,
One morning in the spring.

Clouds sail over the distant trees,
Petals are shaken down by the breeze,
They fall on the terrace tiles like snow;
The sighing of waves sounds, far below.
A humming-bird kisses the lips of a rose
Then laden with honey and love he goes.
The minstrel woos with his silver strings,
And climbing up to the lady, sings:—
    Down the road to Avignon,
    The long, long road to Avignon,
    Across the bridge to Avignon,
    One morning in the spring.

Step by step, and he comes to her,
Fearful lest she suddenly stir.
Sunshine and silence, and each to each,
The lute and his singing their only speech;
He leans above her, her eyes unclose,
The humming-bird enters another rose.
The minstrel hushes his silver strings.
Hark! The beating of humming-birds' wings!
    Down the road to Avignon,
    The long, long road to Avignon,
    Across the bridge to Avignon,
    One morning in the spring.

AMY LOWELL

New York at Night

A near horizon whose sharp jags
    Cut brutally into a sky
Of leaden heaviness, and crags
Of houses lift their masonry
    Ugly and foul, and chimneys lie
And snort, outlined against the gray
    Of lowhung cloud. I hear the sigh
The goaded city gives, not day
Nor night can ease her heart, her anguished labours stay.

Below, straight streets, monotonous,
    From north and south, from east and west,
Stretch glittering; and luminous
    Above, one tower tops the rest
    And holds aloft man's constant quest:
Time! Joyless emblem of the greed
    Of millions, robber of the best
Which earth can give, the vulgar creed
Has seared upon the night its flaming ruthless screed.

O Night! Whose soothing presence brings
    The quiet shining of the stars.
O Night! Whose cloak of darkness clings
    So intimately close that scars
    Are hid from our own eyes. Beggars
By day, our wealth is having night
    To burn our souls before altars
Dim and tree-shadowed, where the light
Is shed from a young moon, mysteriously bright.

Where art thou hiding, where thy peace?
    This is the hour, but thou art not.
Will waking tumult never cease?
    Hast thou thy votary forgot?
    Nature forsakes this man-begot

And festering wilderness, and now
    The long still hours are here, no jot
Of dear communing do I know;
Instead the glaring, man-filled city groans below!

A Fairy Tale

On winter nights beside the nursery fire
We read the fairy tale, while glowing coals
Builded its pictures. There before our eyes
We saw the vaulted hall of traceried stone
Uprear itself, the distant ceiling hung
With pendent stalactites like frozen vines;
And all along the walls at intervals,
Curled upwards into pillars, roses climbed,
And ramped and were confined, and clustered leaves
Divided where there peered a laughing face.
The foliage seemed to rustle in the wind,
A silent murmur, carved in still, gray stone.
High pointed windows pierced the southern wall
Whence proud escutcheons flung prismatic fires
To stain the tessellated marble floor
With pools of red, and quivering green, and blue;
And in the shade beyond the further door,
Its sober squares of black and white were hid
Beneath a restless, shuffling, wide-eyed mob
Of lackeys and retainers come to view
The Christening.
A sudden blare of trumpets, and the throng
About the entrance parted as the guests
Filed singly in with rare and precious gifts.
Our eager fancies noted all they brought,
The glorious, unattainable delights!
But always there was one unbidden guest
Who cursed the child and left it bitterness.

The fire falls asunder, all is changed,
I am no more a child, and what I see
Is not a fairy tale, but life, my life.
The gifts are there, the many pleasant things:
Health, wealth, long-settled friendships, with a name
Which honors all who bear it, and the power
Of making words obedient. This is much;

But overshadowing all is still the curse,
That never shall I be fulfilled by love!
Along the parching highroad of the world
No other soul shall bear mine company.
Always shall I be teased with semblances,
With cruel impostures, which I trust awhile
Then dash to pieces, as a careless boy
Flings a kaleidoscope, which shattering
Strews all the ground about with coloured sherds.
So I behold my visions on the ground
No longer radiant, an ignoble heap
Of broken, dusty glass. And so, unlit,
Even by hope or faith, my dragging steps
Force me forever through the passing days.

CROWNED

You came to me bearing bright roses,
　　Red like the wine of your heart;
You twisted them into a garland
　　To set me aside from the mart.
Red roses to crown me your lover,
　　And I walked aureoled and apart.

Enslaved and encircled, I bore it,
　　Proud token of my gift to you.
The petals waned paler, and shriveled,
　　And dropped; and the thorns started through.
Bitter thorns to proclaim me your lover,
　　A diadem woven with rue.

TO ELIZABETH WARD PERKINS

Dear Bessie, would my tired rhyme
    Had force to rise from apathy,
    And shaking off its lethargy
Ring word-tones like a Christmas chime.

But in my soul's high belfry, chill
    The bitter wind of doubt has blown,
    The summer swallows all have flown,
The bells are frost-bound, mute and still.

Upon the crumbling boards the snow
    Has drifted deep, the clappers hang
    Prismed with icicles, their clang
Unheard since ages long ago.

The rope I pull is stiff and cold,
    My straining ears detect no sound
    Except a sigh, as round and round
The wind rocks through the timbers old.

Below, I know the church is bright
    With haloed tapers, warm with prayer;
    But here I only feel the air
Of icy centuries of night.

Beneath my feet the snow is lit
    And gemmed with colours, red, and blue,
    Topaz, and green, where light falls through
The saints that in the windows sit.

Here darkness seems a spectred thing,
    Voiceless and haunting, while the stars
    Mock with a light of long dead years
The ache of present suffering.

Silent and winter-killed I stand,
    No carol hymns my debt to you;
    But take this frozen thought in lieu,
And thaw its music in your hand.

The Promise of the Morning Star

Thou father of the children of my brain
    By thee engendered in my willing heart,
    How can I thank thee for this gift of art
Poured out so lavishly, and not in vain.

What thou created never more can die,
    Thy fructifying power lives in me
    And I conceive, knowing it is by thee,
Dear other parent of my poetry!

For I was but a shadow with a name,
    Perhaps by now the very name's forgot;
    So strange is Fate that it has been my lot
To learn through thee the presence of that aim

Which evermore must guide me. All unknown,
    By me unguessed, by thee not even dreamed,
    A tree has blossomed in a night that seemed
Of stubborn, barren wood. For thou hast sown

This seed of beauty in a ground of truth.
    Humbly I dedicate myself, and yet
    I tremble with a sudden fear to set
New music ringing through my fading youth.

J—K. Huysmans

A flickering glimmer through a window-pane,
A dim red glare through mud bespattered glass,
Cleaving a path between blown walls of sleet
Across uneven pavements sunk in slime
To scatter and then quench itself in mist.
And struggling, slipping, often rudely hurled
Against the jutting angle of a wall,
And cursed, and reeled against, and flung aside
By drunken brawlers as they shuffled past,
A man was groping to what seemed a light.
His eyelids burnt and quivered with the strain
Of looking, and against his temples beat
The all enshrouding, suffocating dark.
He stumbled, lurched, and struck against a door
That opened, and a howl of obscene mirth
Grated his senses, wallowing on the floor
Lay men, and dogs and women in the dirt.
He sickened, loathing it, and as he gazed
The candle guttered, flared, and then went out.

Through travail of ignoble midnight streets
He came at last to shelter in a porch
Where gothic saints and warriors made a shield
To cover him, and tortured gargoyles spat
One long continuous stream of silver rain
That clattered down from myriad roofs and spires
Into a darkness, loud with rushing sound
Of water falling, gurgling as it fell,
But always thickly dark. Then as he leaned
Unconscious where, the great oak door blew back
And cast him, bruised and dripping, in the church.
His eyes from long sojourning in the night
Were blinded now as by some glorious sun;
He slowly crawled toward the altar steps.
He could not think, for heavy in his ears

An organ boomed majestic harmonies;
He only knew that what he saw was light!
He bowed himself before a cross of flame
And shut his eyes in fear lest it should fade.

March Evening

Blue through the window burns the twilight;
    Heavy, through trees, blows the warm south wind.
Glistening, against the chill, gray sky light,
    Wet, black branches are barred and entwined.

Sodden and spongy, the scarce-green grass plot
    Dents into pools where a foot has been.
Puddles lie spilt in the road a mass, not
    Of water, but steel, with its cold, hard sheen.

Faint fades the fire on the hearth, its embers
    Scattering wide at a stronger gust.
Above, the old weathercock groans, but remembers
    Creaking, to turn, in its centuried rust.

Dying, forlorn, in dreary sorrow,
    Wrapping the mists round her withering form,
Day sinks down; and in darkness tomorrow
    Travails to birth in the womb of the storm.

SONNETS

LEISURE

Leisure, thou goddess of a bygone age,
    When hours were long and days sufficed to hold
    Wide-eyed delights and pleasures uncontrolled
By shortening moments, when no gaunt presage
Of undone duties, modern heritage,
    Haunted our happy minds; must thou withhold
    Thy presence from this over-busy world,
And bearing silence with thee disengage
    Our twined fortunes? Deeps of unhewn woods
    Alone can cherish thee, alone possess
Thy quiet, teeming vigor. This our crime:
    Not to have worshipped, marred by alien moods
    That sole condition of all loveliness,
The dreaming lapse of slow, unmeasured time.

On Carpaccio's Picture:
The Dream of St. Ursula

Swept, clean, and still, across the polished floor
  From some unshuttered casement, hid from sight,
  The level sunshine slants, its greater light
Quenching the little lamp which pallid, poor,
Flickering, unreplenished, at the door
  Has striven against darkness the long night.
  Dawn fills the room, and penetrating, bright,
The silent sunbeams through the window pour.
  And she lies sleeping, ignorant of Fate,
  Enmeshed in listless dreams, her soul not yet
Ripened to bear the purport of this day.
  The morning breeze scarce stirs the coverlet,
  A shadow falls across the sunlight; wait!
A lark is singing as he flies away.

The Matrix

Goaded and harassed in the factory
    That tears our life up into bits of days
    Ticked off upon a clock which never stays,
Shredding our portion of Eternity,
We break away at last, and steal the key
    Which hides a world empty of hours; ways
    Of space unroll, and Heaven overlays
The leafy, sun-lit earth of Fantasy.
    Beyond the ilex shadow glares the sun,
    Scorching against the blue flame of the sky.
Brown lily-pads lie heavy and supine
    Within a granite basin, under one
    The bronze-gold glimmer of a carp; and I
Reach out my hand and pluck a nectarine.

Monadnock in Early Spring

Cloud-topped and splendid, dominating all
    The little lesser hills which compass thee,
    Thou standest, bright with April's buoyancy,
Yet holding Winter in some shaded wall
Of stern, steep rock; and startled by the call
    Of Spring, thy trees flush with expectancy
    And cast a cloud of crimson, silently,
Above thy snowy crevices where fall
    Pale shrivelled oak leaves, while the snow beneath
    Melts at their phantom touch. Another year
Is quick with import. Such each year has been.
    Unmoved thou watchest all, and all bequeath
    Some jewel to thy diadem of power,
Thou pledge of greater majesty unseen.

The Little Garden

A little garden on a bleak hillside
    Where deep the heavy, dazzling mountain snow
    Lies far into the spring. The sun's pale glow
Is scarcely able to melt patches wide
About the single rose bush. All denied
    Of nature's tender ministries. But no,—
    For wonder-working faith has made it blow
With flowers many hued and starry-eyed.
    Here sleeps the sun long, idle summer hours;
Here butterflies and bees fare far to rove
    Amid the crumpled leaves of poppy flowers;
Here four o'clocks, to the passionate night above
    Fling whiffs of perfume, like pale incense showers.
A little garden, loved with a great love!

To an Early Daffodil

Thou yellow trumpeter of laggard Spring!
    Thou herald of rich Summer's myriad flowers!
    The climbing sun with new recovered powers
Does warm thee into being, through the ring
Of rich, brown earth he woos thee, makes thee fling
    Thy green shoots up, inheriting the dowers
    Of bending sky and sudden, sweeping showers,
Till ripe and blossoming thou art a thing
    To make all nature glad, thou art so gay;
To fill the lonely with a joy untold;
    Nodding at every gust of wind today,
Tomorrow jewelled with raindrops. Always bold
    To stand erect, full in the dazzling play
Of April's sun, for thou hast caught his gold.

LISTENING

'T is you that are the music, not your song.
    The song is but a door which, opening wide,
    Lets forth the pent-up melody inside,
Your spirit's harmony, which clear and strong
Sings but of you. Throughout your whole life long
    Your songs, your thoughts, your doings, each divide
    This perfect beauty; waves within a tide,
Or single notes amid a glorious throng.
    The song of earth has many different chords;
Ocean has many moods and many tones
    Yet always ocean. In the damp Spring woods
The painted trillium smiles, while crisp pine cones
    Autumn alone can ripen. So is this
    One music with a thousand cadences.

THE LAMP OF LIFE

Always we are following a light,
    Always the light recedes; with groping hands
    We stretch toward this glory, while the lands
We journey through are hidden from our sight
Dim and mysterious, folded deep in night,
    We care not, all our utmost need demands
    Is but the light, the light! So still it stands
Surely our own if we exert our might.
Fool! Never can'st thou grasp this fleeting gleam,
    Its glowing flame would die if it were caught,
Its value is that it doth always seem
    But just a little farther on. Distraught,
    But lighted ever onward, we are brought
Upon our way unknowing, in a dream.

Hero-Worship

A face seen passing in a crowded street,
 A voice heard singing music, large and free;
 And from that moment life is changed, and we
Become of more heroic temper, meet
To freely ask and give, a man complete
 Radiant because of faith, we dare to be
 What Nature meant us. Brave idolatry
Which can conceive a hero! No deceit,
 No knowledge taught by unrelenting years,
 Can quench this fierce, untamable desire.
We know that what we long for once achieved
 Will cease to satisfy. Be still our fears;
 If what we worship fail us, still the fire
Burns on, and it is much to have believed.

In Darkness

Must all of worth be travailled for, and those
    Life's brightest stars rise from a troubled sea?
    Must years go by in sad uncertainty
Leaving us doubting whose the conquering blows,
Are we or Fate the victors? Time which shows
    All inner meanings will reveal, but we
    Shall never know the upshot. Ours to be
Wasted with longing, shattered in the throes,
    The agonies of splendid dreams, which day
    Dims from our vision, but each night brings back;
We strive to hold their grandeur, and essay
    To be the thing we dream. Sudden we lack
The flash of insight, life grows drear and gray,
    And hour follows hour, nerveless, slack.

Before Dawn

Life! Austere arbiter of each man's fate,
    By whom he learns that Nature's steadfast laws
    Are as decrees immutable; O pause
Your even forward march! Not yet too late
Teach me the needed lesson, when to wait
    Inactive as a ship when no wind draws
    To stretch the loosened cordage. One implores
Thy clemency, whose wilfulness innate
        Has gone uncurbed and roughshod while the years
                Have lengthened into decades; now distressed
He knows no rule by which to move or stay,
    And teased with restlessness and desperate fears
He dares not watch in silence thy wise way
                Bringing about results none could have guessed.

THE POET

What instinct forces man to journey on,
    Urged by a longing blind but dominant!
    Nothing he sees can hold him, nothing daunt
His never failing eagerness. The sun
Setting in splendour every night has won
    His vassalage; those towers flamboyant
    Of airy cloudland palaces now haunt
His daylight wanderings. Forever done
With simple joys and quiet happiness
    He guards the vision of the sunset sky;
Though faint with weariness he must possess
    Some fragment of the sunset's majesty;
He spurns life's human friendships to profess
    Life's loneliness of dreaming ecstasy.

AMY LOWELL

At Night

The wind is singing through the trees tonight,
    A deep-voiced song of rushing cadences
    And crashing intervals. No summer breeze
Is this, though hot July is at its height,
Gone is her gentler music; with delight
    She listens to this booming like the seas,
    These elemental, loud necessities
Which call to her to answer their swift might.
    Above the tossing trees shines down a star,
    Quietly bright; this wild, tumultuous joy
Quickens nor dims its splendour. And my mind,
    O Star! is filled with your white light, from far,
    So suffer me this one night to enjoy
The freedom of the onward sweeping wind.

The Fruit Garden Path

The path runs straight between the flowering rows,
    A moonlit path, hemmed in by beds of bloom,
    Where phlox and marigolds dispute for room
With tall, red dahlias and the briar rose.
'T is reckless prodigality which throws
    Into the night these wafts of rich perfume
    Which sweep across the garden like a plume.
Over the trees a single bright star glows.
    Dear garden of my childhood, here my years
Have run away like little grains of sand;
    The moments of my life, its hopes and fears
Have all found utterance here, where now I stand;
    My eyes ache with the weight of unshed tears,
You are my home, do you not understand?

AMY LOWELL

Mirage

How is it that, being gone, you fill my days,
    And all the long nights are made glad by thee?
    No loneliness is this, nor misery,
But great content that these should be the ways
Whereby the Fancy, dreaming as she strays,
    Makes bright and present what she would would be.
    And who shall say if the reality
Is not with dreams so pregnant. For delays
    And hindrances may bar the wished-for end;
A thousand misconceptions may prevent
    Our souls from coming near enough to blend;
Let me but think we have the same intent,
    That each one needs to call the other, "friend!"
It may be vain illusion. I'm content.

To a Friend

I ask but one thing of you, only one,
    That always you will be my dream of you;
    That never shall I wake to find untrue
All this I have believed and rested on,
Forever vanished, like a vision gone
    Out into the night. Alas, how few
    There are who strike in us a chord we knew
Existed, but so seldom heard its tone
    We tremble at the half-forgotten sound.
The world is full of rude awakenings
    And heaven-born castles shattered to the ground,
Yet still our human longing vainly clings
    To a belief in beauty through all wrongs.
    O stay your hand, and leave my heart its songs!

A Fixed Idea

What torture lurks within a single thought
When grown too constant, and however kind,
However welcome still, the weary mind
Aches with its presence. Dull remembrance taught
Remembers on unceasingly; unsought
The old delight is with us but to find
That all recurring joy is pain refined,
Become a habit, and we struggle, caught.
You lie upon my heart as on a nest,
Folded in peace, for you can never know
How crushed I am with having you at rest
Heavy upon my life. I love you so
You bind my freedom from its rightful quest.
In mercy lift your drooping wings and go.

Dreams

I do not care to talk to you although
    Your speech evokes a thousand sympathies,
    And all my being's silent harmonies
Wake trembling into music. When you go
It is as if some sudden, dreadful blow
    Had severed all the strings with savage ease.
    No, do not talk; but let us rather seize
This intimate gift of silence which we know.
    Others may guess your thoughts from what you say,
As storms are guessed from clouds where darkness broods.
    To me the very essence of the day
Reveals its inner purpose and its moods;
    As poplars feel the rain and then straightway
Reverse their leaves and shimmer through the woods.

Frankincense and Myrrh

My heart is tuned to sorrow, and the strings
   Vibrate most readily to minor chords,
   Searching and sad; my mind is stuffed with words
Which voice the passion and the ache of things:
Illusions beating with their baffled wings
   Against the walls of circumstance, and hoards
   Of torn desires, broken joys; records
Of all a bruised life's maimed imaginings.
   Now you are come! You tremble like a star
Poised where, behind earth's rim, the sun has set.
      Your voice has sung across my heart, but numb
   And mute, I have no tones to answer. Far
Within I kneel before you, speechless yet,
      And life ablaze with beauty, I am dumb.

From One Who Stays

How empty seems the town now you are gone!
    A wilderness of sad streets, where gaunt walls
    Hide nothing to desire; sunshine falls
Eery, distorted, as it long had shone
On white, dead faces tombed in halls of stone.
    The whir of motors, stricken through with calls
    Of playing boys, floats up at intervals;
But all these noises blur to one long moan.
    What quest is worth pursuing? And how strange
That other men still go accustomed ways!
        I hate their interest in the things they do.
    A spectre-horde repeating without change
An old routine. Alone I know the days
        Are still-born, and the world stopped, lacking you.

CREPUSCULE DU MATIN

All night I wrestled with a memory
    Which knocked insurgent at the gates of thought.
    The crumbled wreck of years behind has wrought
Its disillusion; now I only cry
For peace, for power to forget the lie
    Which hope too long has whispered. So I sought
    The sleep which would not come, and night was fraught
With old emotions weeping silently.
I heard your voice again, and knew the things
    Which you had promised proved an empty vaunt.
I felt your clinging hands while night's broad wings
Cherished our love in darkness. From the lawn
    A sudden, quivering birdnote, like a taunt.
My arms held nothing but the empty dawn.

Aftermath

I learnt to write to you in happier days,
    And every letter was a piece I chipped
    From off my heart, a fragment newly clipped
From the mosaic of life; its blues and grays,
Its throbbing reds, I gave to earn your praise.
    To make a pavement for your feet I stripped
    My soul for you to walk upon, and slipped
Beneath your steps to soften all your ways.
    But now my letters are like blossoms pale
We strew upon a grave with hopeless tears.
    I ask no recompense, I shall not fail
Although you do not heed; the long, sad years
    Still pass, and still I scatter flowers frail,
And whisper words of love which no one hears.

AMY LOWELL

THE END

Throughout the echoing chambers of my brain
    I hear your words in mournful cadence toll
    Like some slow passing-bell which warns the soul
Of sundering darkness. Unrelenting, fain
To batter down resistance, fall again
    Stroke after stroke, insistent diastole,
    The bitter blows of truth, until the whole
Is hammered into fact made strangely plain.
    Where shall I look for comfort? Not to you.
        Our worlds are drawn apart, our spirit's suns
Divided, and the light of mine burnt dim.
    Now in the haunted twilight I must do
        Your will. I grasp the cup which over-runs,
And with my trembling lips I touch the rim.

The Starling

"'I can't get out', said the starling."

—Sterne's 'Sentimental Journey'

Forever the impenetrable wall
    Of self confines my poor rebellious soul,
    I never see the towering white clouds roll
Before a sturdy wind, save through the small
Barred window of my jail. I live a thrall
    With all my outer life a clipped, square hole,
    Rectangular; a fraction of a scroll
Unwound and winding like a worsted ball.
    My thoughts are grown uneager and depressed
        Through being always mine, my fancy's wings
Are moulted and the feathers blown away.
    I weary for desires never guessed,
        For alien passions, strange imaginings,
To be some other person for a day.

Market Day

White, glittering sunlight fills the market square,
  Spotted and sprigged with shadows. Double rows
  Of bartering booths spread out their tempting shows
Of globed and golden fruit, the morning air
Smells sweet with ripeness, on the pavement there
  A wicker basket gapes and overflows
  Spilling out cool, blue plums. The market glows,
And flaunts, and clatters in its busy care.
  A stately minster at the northern side
Lifts its twin spires to the distant sky,
  Pinnacled, carved and buttressed; through the wide
Arched doorway peals an organ, suddenly—
  Crashing, triumphant in its pregnant tide,
Quenching the square in vibrant harmony.

Epitaph in a Church-Yard in Charleston, South Carolina

George Augustus Clough
A Native of Liverpool,
Died Suddenly of "Stranger's Fever"
Nov'r 5th 1843
Aged 22

He died of "Stranger's Fever" when his youth
    Had scarcely melted into manhood, so
    The chiselled legend runs; a brother's woe
Laid bare for epitaph. The savage ruth
Of a sunny, bright, but alien land, uncouth
    With cruel caressing dealt a mortal blow,
    And by this summer sea where flowers grow
In tropic splendor, witness to the truth
Of ineradicable race he lies.
    The law of duty urged that he should roam,
Should sail from fog and chilly airs to skies
    Clear with deceitful welcome. He had come
With proud resolve, but still his lonely eyes
    Ached with fatigue at never seeing home.

AMY LOWELL

Francis II, King of Naples

Written after reading Trevelyan's
"Garibaldi and the making of Italy"

Poor foolish monarch, vacillating, vain,
 Decaying victim of a race of kings,
 Swift Destiny shook out her purple wings
And caught him in their shadow; not again
Could furtive plotting smear another stain
 Across his tarnished honour. Smoulderings
 Of sacrificial fires burst their rings
And blotted out in smoke his lost domain.
Bereft of courtiers, only with his queen,
 From empty palace down to empty quay.
No challenge screamed from hostile carabine.
 A single vessel waited, shadowy;
 All night she ploughed her solitary way
Beneath the stars, and through a tranquil sea.

To John Keats

Great master! Boyish, sympathetic man!
  Whose orbed and ripened genius lightly hung
  From life's slim, twisted tendril and there swung
In crimson-sphered completeness; guardian
Of crystal portals through whose openings fan
  The spiced winds which blew when earth was young,
  Scattering wreaths of stars, as Jove once flung
A golden shower from heights cerulean.
  Crumbled before thy majesty we bow.
    Forget thy empurpled state, thy panoply
Of greatness, and be merciful and near;
  A youth who trudged the highroad we tread now
    Singing the miles behind him; so may we
Faint throbbings of thy music overhear.

THE BOSTON ATHENAEUM

THE BOSTON ATHENAEUM

Thou dear and well-loved haunt of happy hours,
How often in some distant gallery,
Gained by a little painful spiral stair,
Far from the halls and corridors where throng
The crowd of casual readers, have I passed
Long, peaceful hours seated on the floor
Of some retired nook, all lined with books,
Where reverie and quiet reign supreme!
Above, below, on every side, high shelved
From careless grasp of transient interest,
Stand books we can but dimly see, their charm
Much greater that their titles are unread;
While on a level with the dusty floor
Others are ranged in orderly confusion,
And we must stoop in painful posture while
We read their names and learn their histories.
The little gallery winds round about
The middle of a most secluded room,
Midway between the ceiling and the floor.
A type of those high thoughts, which while we read
Hover between the earth and furthest heaven
As fancy wills, leaving the printed page;
For books but give the theme, our hearts the rest,
Enriching simple words with unguessed harmony
And overtones of thought we only know.
And as we sit long hours quietly,
Reading at times, and at times simply dreaming,
The very room itself becomes a friend,
The confidant of intimate hopes and fears;
A place where are engendered pleasant thoughts,
And possibilities before unguessed
Come to fruition born of sympathy.
And as in some gay garden stretched upon
A genial southern slope, warmed by the sun,
The flowers give their fragrance joyously
To the caressing touch of the hot noon;

So books give up the all of what they mean
Only in a congenial atmosphere,
Only when touched by reverent hands, and read
By those who love and feel as well as think.
For books are more than books, they are the life,
The very heart and core of ages past,
The reason why men lived, and worked, and died,
The essence and quintessence of their lives.
And we may know them better, and divine
The inner motives whence their actions sprang,
Far better than the men who only knew
Their bodily presence, the soul forever hid
From those with no ability to see.
They wait here quietly for us to come
And find them out, and know them for our friends;
These men who toiled and wrote only for this,
To leave behind such modicum of truth
As each perceived and each alone could tell.
Silently waiting that from time to time
It may be given them to illuminate
Dull daily facts with pristine radiance
For some long-waited-for affinity
Who lingers yet in the deep womb of time.
The shifting sun pierces the young green leaves
Of elm trees, newly coming into bud,
And splashes on the floor and on the books
Through old, high, rounded windows, dim with age.
The noisy city-sounds of modern life
Float softened to us across the old graveyard.
The room is filled with a warm, mellow light,
No garish colours jar on our content,
The books upon the shelves are old and worn.
'T was no belated effort nor attempt
To keep abreast with old as well as new
That placed them here, tricked in a modern guise,
Easily got, and held in light esteem.
Our fathers' fathers, slowly and carefully
Gathered them, one by one, when they were new
And a delighted world received their thoughts

Hungrily; while we but love the more,
Because they are so old and grown so dear!
The backs of tarnished gold, the faded boards,
The slightly yellowing page, the strange old type,
All speak the fashion of another age;
The thoughts peculiar to the man who wrote
Arrayed in garb peculiar to the time;
As though the idiom of a man were caught
Imprisoned in the idiom of a race.
A nothing truly, yet a link that binds
All ages to their own inheritance,
And stretching backward, dim and dimmer still,
Is lost in a remote antiquity.
Grapes do not come of thorns nor figs of thistles,
And even a great poet's divinest thought
Is coloured by the world he knows and sees.
The little intimate things of every day,
The trivial nothings that we think not of,
These go to make a part of each man's life;
As much a part as do the larger thoughts
He takes account of. Nay, the little things
Of daily life it is which mold, and shape,
And make him apt for noble deeds and true.
And as we read some much-loved masterpiece,
Read it as long ago the author read,
With eyes that brimmed with tears as he saw
The message he believed in stamped in type
Inviolable for the slow-coming years;
We know a certain subtle sympathy,
We seem to clasp his hand across the past,
His words become related to the time,
He is at one with his own glorious creed
And all that in his world was dared and done.
The long, still, fruitful hours slip away
Shedding their influences as they pass;
We know ourselves the richer to have sat
Upon this dusty floor and dreamed our dreams.
No other place to us were quite the same,
No other dreams so potent in their charm,

For this is ours! Every twist and turn
Of every narrow stair is known and loved;
Each nook and cranny is our very own;
The dear, old, sleepy place is full of spells
For us, by right of long inheritance.
The building simply bodies forth a thought
Peculiarly inherent to the race.
And we, descendants of that elder time,
Have learnt to love the very form in which
The thought has been embodied to our years.
And here we feel that we are not alone,
We too are one with our own richest past;
And here that veiled, but ever smouldering fire
Of race, which rarely seen yet never dies,
Springs up afresh and warms us with its heat.
And must they take away this treasure house,
To us so full of thoughts and memories;
To all the world beside a dismal place
Lacking in all this modern age requires
To tempt along the unfamiliar paths
And leafy lanes of old time literatures?
It takes some time for moss and vines to grow
And warmly cover gaunt and chill stone walls
Of stately buildings from the cold North Wind.
The lichen of affection takes as long,
Or longer, ere it lovingly enfolds
A place which since without it were bereft,
All stript and bare, shorn of its chiefest grace.
For what to us were halls and corridors
However large and fitting, if we part
With this which is our birthright; if we lose
A sentiment profound, unsoundable,
Which Time's slow ripening alone can make,
And man's blind foolishness so quickly mar.

AMY LOWELL

VERSES FOR CHILDREN

Sea Shell

Sea Shell, Sea Shell,
    Sing me a song, O Please!
A song of ships, and sailor men,
    And parrots, and tropical trees,

Of islands lost in the Spanish Main
Which no man ever may find again,
Of fishes and corals under the waves,
And seahorses stabled in great green caves.

Sea Shell, Sea Shell,
Sing of the things you know so well.

Fringed Gentians

Near where I live there is a lake
As blue as blue can be, winds make
It dance as they go blowing by.
I think it curtseys to the sky.

It's just a lake of lovely flowers
And my Mamma says they are ours;
But they are not like those we grow
To be our very own, you know.

We have a splendid garden, there
Are lots of flowers everywhere;
Roses, and pinks, and four o'clocks
And hollyhocks, and evening stocks.

Mamma lets us pick them, but never
Must we pick any gentians—ever!
For if we carried them away
They'd die of homesickness that day.

AMY LOWELL

The Painted Ceiling

My Grandpapa lives in a wonderful house
    With a great many windows and doors,
There are stairs that go up, and stairs that go down,
    And such beautiful, slippery floors.

But of all of the rooms, even mother's and mine,
    And the bookroom, and parlour and all,
I like the green dining-room so much the best
    Because of its ceiling and wall.

Right over your head is a funny round hole
    With apples and pears falling through;
There's a big bunch of grapes all purply and sweet,
    And melons and pineapples too.

They tumble and tumble, but never come down
    Though I've stood underneath a long while
With my mouth open wide, for I always have hoped
    Just a cherry would drop from the pile.

No matter how early I run there to look
    It has always begun to fall through;
And one night when at bedtime I crept in to see,
    It was falling by candle-light too.

I am sure they are magical fruits, and each one
    Makes you hear things, or see things, or go
Forever invisible; but it's no use,
    And of course I shall just never know.

For the ladder's too heavy to lift, and the chairs
    Are not nearly so tall as I need.
I've given up hope, and I feel I shall die
    Without having accomplished the deed.

It's a little bit sad, when you seem very near
    To adventures and things of that sort,
Which nearly begin, and then don't; and you know
    It is only because you are short.

THE CRESCENT MOON

Slipping softly through the sky
    Little horned, happy moon,
Can you hear me up so high?
    Will you come down soon?

On my nursery window-sill
    Will you stay your steady flight?
And then float away with me
    Through the summer night?

Brushing over tops of trees,
    Playing hide and seek with stars,
Peeping up through shiny clouds
    At Jupiter or Mars.

I shall fill my lap with roses
    Gathered in the milky way,
All to carry home to mother.
    Oh! what will she say!

Little rocking, sailing moon,
    Do you hear me shout—Ahoy!
Just a little nearer, moon,
    To please a little boy.

CLIMBING

High up in the apple tree climbing I go,
With the sky above me, the earth below.
Each branch is the step of a wonderful stair
Which leads to the town I see shining up there.

Climbing, climbing, higher and higher,
The branches blow and I see a spire,
The gleam of a turret, the glint of a dome,
All sparkling and bright, like white sea foam.

On and on, from bough to bough,
The leaves are thick, but I push my way through;
Before, I have always had to stop,
But today I am sure I shall reach the top.

Today to the end of the marvelous stair,
Where those glittering pinacles flash in the air!
Climbing, climbing, higher I go,
With the sky close above me, the earth far below.

AMY LOWELL

THE TROUT

Naughty little speckled trout,
Can't I coax you to come out?
Is it such great fun to play
In the water every day?

Do you pull the Naiads' hair
Hiding in the lilies there?
Do you hunt for fishes' eggs,
Or watch tadpoles grow their legs?

Do the little trouts have school
In some deep sun-glinted pool,
And in recess play at tag
Round that bed of purple flag?

I have tried so hard to catch you,
Hours and hours I've sat to watch you;
But you never will come out,
Naughty little speckled trout!

Wind

He shouts in the sails of the ships at sea,
He steals the down from the honeybee,
He makes the forest trees rustle and sing,
He twirls my kite till it breaks its string.
    Laughing, dancing, sunny wind,
    Whistling, howling, rainy wind,
    North, South, East and West,
    Each is the wind I like the best.

He calls up the fog and hides the hills,
He whirls the wings of the great windmills,
The weathercocks love him and turn to discover
His whereabouts—but he's gone, the rover!
    Laughing, dancing, sunny wind,
    Whistling, howling, rainy wind,
    North, South, East and West,
    Each is the wind I like the best.

The pine trees toss him their cones with glee,
The flowers bend low in courtesy,
Each wave flings up a shower of pearls,
The flag in front of the school unfurls.
    Laughing, dancing, sunny wind,
    Whistling, howling, rainy wind,
    North, South, East and West,
    Each is the wind I like the best

THE PLEIADES

By day you cannot see the sky
For it is up so very high.
You look and look, but it's so blue
That you can never see right through.

But when night comes it is quite plain,
And all the stars are there again.
They seem just like old friends to me,
I've known them all my life you see.

There is the dipper first, and there
Is Cassiopeia in her chair,
Orion's belt, the Milky Way,
And lots I know but cannot say.

One group looks like a swarm of bees,
Papa says they're the Pleiades;
But I think they must be the toy
Of some nice little angel boy.

Perhaps his jackstones which today
He has forgot to put away,
And left them lying on the sky
Where he will find them bye and bye.

I wish he'd come and play with me.
We'd have such fun, for it would be
A most unusual thing for boys
To feel that they had stars for toys!

THE END

A Note About the Author

Amy Lowell (1874–1925) was an American poet. Born into an elite family of businessmen, politicians, and intellectuals, Lowell was a member of the so-called Boston Brahmin class. She excelled in school from a young age and developed a habit for reading and book collecting. Denied the opportunity to attend college by her family, Lowell traveled extensively in her twenties and turned to poetry in 1902. While in England with her lover Ada Dwyer Russell, she met American poet Ezra Pound, whose influence as an imagist and fierce critic of Lowell's work would prove essential to her poetry. In 1912, only two years after publishing her first poem in *The Atlantic Monthly*, Lowell produced *A Dome of Many-Coloured Glass,* her debut volume of poems. In addition to such collections of her own poems as *Sword Blades and Poppy Seed* (1914) and *Men, Women, and Ghosts* (1916), Lowell published translations of 8th century Chinese poet Li Tai-po and, at the time of her death, had been working on a biography of English Romantic John Keats.

A Note from the Publisher

Spanning many genres, from non-fiction essays to literature classics to children's books and lyric poetry, Mint Edition books showcase the master works of our time in a modern new package. The text is freshly typeset, is clean and easy to read, and features a new note about the author in each volume. Many books also include exclusive new introductory material. Every book boasts a striking new cover, which makes it as appropriate for collecting as it is for gift giving. Mint Edition books are only printed when a reader orders them, so natural resources are not wasted. We're proud that our books are never manufactured in excess and exist only in the exact quantity they need to be read and enjoyed.

bookfinity™

Discover more of your favorite classics with Bookfinity™.

- Track your reading with custom book lists.
- Get great book recommendations for your personalized Reader Type.
- Add reviews for your favorite books.
- AND MUCH MORE!

Visit **bookfinity.com** and take the fun Reader Type quiz to get started.

Enjoy our classic and modern companion pairings!

Classic & Modern

Bookfinity is a registered trademark of Ingram Book Group LLC. © 2023 Bookfinity. All rights reserved.